THE FUNGUS BIG GREEN BOGEY BOOK

Based on the character
Fungus the Bogeyman created by

RAYMOND BRIGGS

Written by Richard Dungworth

Illustrated by Rowan Clifford

Puffin

Hullo there, fellow Bogies!
Welcome to my Big Green Bogey Book,
oozing with oodles of foul-smelling fun,
and dripping with deliciously damp decay.

Within these putrid pages you'll find gutbustingly
gross gags, revolting rhymes and bogey-bagfuls
of other sublimely slimy THINGS.

So pour yourself a nice cold slime, put your
fetid feet up, and wallow!

The Fungus Big Green Bogey Book

NOT FOR THE FAINT-HEARTED!

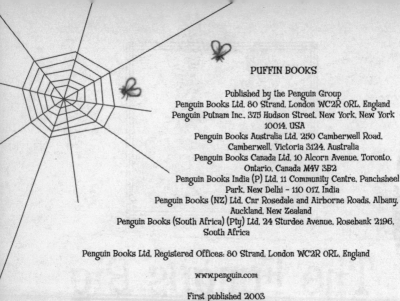

PUFFIN BOOKS

Published by the Penguin Group
Penguin Books Ltd, 80 Strand, London WC2R ORL, England
Penguin Putnam Inc., 375 Hudson Street, New York, New York
10014, USA
Penguin Books Australia Ltd, 250 Camberwell Road,
Camberwell, Victoria 3124, Australia
Penguin Books Canada Ltd, 10 Alcorn Avenue, Toronto,
Ontario, Canada M4V 3B2
Penguin Books India (P) Ltd, 11 Community Centre, Panchsheel
Park, New Delhi – 110 017, India
Penguin Books (NZ) Ltd, Cnr Rosedale and Airborne Roads, Albany,
Auckland, New Zealand
Penguin Books (South Africa) (Pty) Ltd, 24 Sturdee Avenue, Rosebank 2196,
South Africa

Penguin Books Ltd, Registered Offices: 80 Strand, London WC2R ORL, England

www.penguin.com

First published 2003
1 3 5 7 9 10 8 6 4 2

Copyright ©Raymond Briggs, 2003
All rights reserved

The moral right of the author has been asserted

Set in Fink Roman

Made and printed in England by Clays Ltd, St Ives plc

British Library Cataloguing in Publication Data
A CIP catalogue record for this book is available from the British Library

ISBN 0-141-31663-2

WARNING:

FOR BOGEY EYES ONLY.

This book must not be carried Up Top*
at any time. Should it fall into the hands
of a Drycleaner** it will, on being allowed
to dry out, give rise to festering boils
on the faces of all who handle it.

*Over ground
** People who live on the surface

CONTENTS

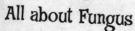

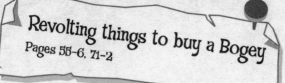
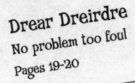

FUNGUS: ALL IS REVEALED

I THOUGHT YOU'D LIKE TO KNOW ALL ABOUT ME ...

Long black tongue used for catching flies and other crunchy creatures

Huge mouth containing 175 blunt, black teeth

Red retractable hair tuft

Huge ears, full of sticky earwax

Rubbery spinal fin

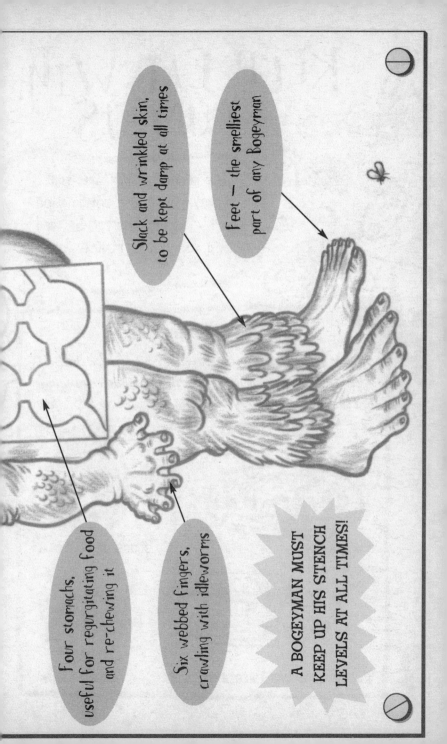

KEEP FAT WITH FUNGUS

The secret of my fine, full Bogey figure is a combination of a rigorous high-fat diet and a strict sloth regime.

FUNGUS'S DIETING TIPS

Stick to greasy foods that are well decayed (check the Best After Date, or look for a good coating of mould or fungus). Eat lots — remember, you've four stomachs to fill. A few keep-fat favourites are:

FETID TRIPE

SLUGS IN AXLE JAM

RIPE EGGS IN TOE-CHEESE SAUCE

EARWAX PATÉ

It's not just what you eat, it's how you eat that makes a difference. Take time to regurgitate your food and have another chew. This will give you the best chance of digesting the precious high-fat mould or fungal growth in your diet.

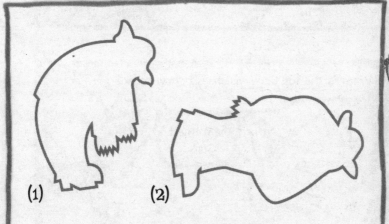

(1)   (2)

EXERCISE – THE GREAT ENEMY

Remember — sloth is the key. An idle Bogey is a happy Bogey. Try to have at least one day a week when you don't get out of bed at all. Avoid unnecessary speed at all costs — less haste, more waist.

It's vital to have a full set of idleworms living under your fingernails at all times. They show that you're living in a suitably idle fashion (they also make a handy snack). Check for them regularly. If they begin to dwindle, slow down and exert yourself less.

What fast food do Bogeymen eat?

Barfburgers with stench flies!

What is the top Bogeyvision quiz show called?

The Weakest Stink.

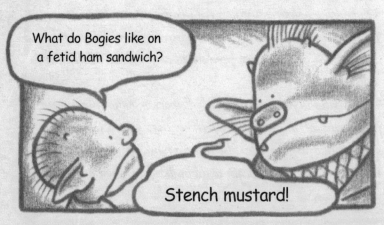

What do Bogies like on a fetid ham sandwich?

Stench mustard!

FETID FLOORS

No micro-life left in your living-room carpet? Kitchen tiles dried out and died out? No bugs in your rugs? Come down to FETID FLOORS for that living floor feel!

FETID fabric floor-coverings are woven from only the most beautifully filthy and matted animal hair. All come ready impregnated with lice-eggs as standard, and can be supplied ready-treated with any of a wide range of long-lasting Stenchseal® odours on request.

Our patented SWAMPGUARD® treatment means that we can guarantee you a floor covering that will stay damp for over 25 years, so you can be sure there'll always be THINGS* squirming underfoot.

If it's linoleum or laminate flooring you need, we can offer an impressive colour range, from grimy green to murky brown, all supplied with an Everwet® permanently sticky finish of your choice (available in slug-trail gloss or grime-smear matt).

WHY NOT DROP IN TO OUR MARSH PARK WAREHOUSE TO TAKE A LOOK – BECAUSE WHATEVER FLOOR YOUR LOOKING FOR, YOU'LL GET IT – AT FETID!

FETID FLOORS –

no floors more filthy, and that's a promise

*THINGS not supplied. Dip into your own Bogey Bag for a few.

MILDEW'S PANTRY

LICE CAKES

Pickled Bunions

FEETYBIX

Sweat Corns

PETIT POOS
– tender rat droppings

SWEAT & SOUR SAUCE

CORNED BARF

Creamed Mice Pudding

FILTH FINGERS
Dead Bird's Eye brand

Filthadelphia
soft toe-cheese spread

Grotdog Sausages

VERMINICELLI
(shredded rat)

Slimefast Shakes
for easy weight gain

CHEWED TUNA
CHUNKS IN BILE

SPAGSWETTI BOGNAISE

A SPOTTER'S GUIDE TO DRYCLEANERS*.

*Humans

The Grimeling, Or 'Teenager'

Often put forward as evidence that the Bogey and Drycleaner races may have interbred at some point in their evolution. This Drycleaner type lives in a respectable degree of filth and stench, and shows promising signs of avoiding sunlight and exercise.

Pus-filled facial 'spots' show some likeness to Bogey neck-boils

The Cleanerator

Under no circumstances approach this creature. She stands for everything anti-Bogey. Armed with a number of diabolical devices used specifically to remove dirt and grime, and a range of horrific chemicals for destroying the delightful smells of decay and waste. She is largely responsible for the revolting cleanliness of the Drycleaners' workplaces and schools.

Typical Cleanerator's equipment, including a frightful nozzled 'dirtsucker' device

14

ODIOUS ODES

TO MY BOGEY GIRLFRIEND

Shall I compare thee to a winter's day?
Thou art more grey and soggy.
Thy ugliness is without match,
Thy reek makes me feel groggy
Thy feet so ripe, like ancient cheese,
Thy underarms so rancid,
Thou truly art, my Bogey Drear,
The One I've always fancied.

I

AN ODE TO SLIME

Sometimes thou hast a yellow hue
Sometimes thou art more green
Thou always hast a nasty smell
And are pleasingly unclean.
Sometimes sloppy, sometimes slimy,
Thou always taste divine
And as an extra special treat
Add a double dose of grime.

II

DREAR DREIRDRE
NO PROBLEM TOO FOUL

Drear Dreirdre
My teachers and parents are giving me a hard time because I won't eat my school dinners. But the meals they dish up are horrid — the food barely smells, and sometimes it's quite obviously not even rotten yet — revolting. Last week they gave us cabbage with NO SLUGS OR CATERPILLARS IN IT WHATSOEVER. What can I do?

CRUDELIA, AGED 8

Dreirdre says...

Drear Crudelia
Your school meals sound truly awful. Perhaps there's a new dinner lady who hasn't learned to let the food rot properly yet? Try having a word with your head teacher. Or ask your mum if she'll make some putrid packed lunches for you. Packing up a

lunch a **few weeks** in advance **is** a great way to **ensure** that it's got **plenty** of **flavour** and stench by **the time** you come to eat it.

Drear Dreirdre

I've been suffering for some time now with an embarrassing health problem. Whenever I'm out in public, I lose the ability to belch or break wind. I've seen several specialists, but to no avail. Can you help?

B.O., AGED 11

DREIRDRE SAYS...

Drear B.O.

I **suspect your problem** is **partly due** to **nerves,** and **partly** to **insufficient methane** in **your diet.** Make **sure** that **you eat** lots of **rotten eggs** and **putrid vegetables,** and **try** to **stay calm** and **relaxed, particularly** from **the waist down,** when you go out — you'll soon be farting like a foghorn again.

FUNGUS'S SCRATCH 'N' SNIFF SMELLING TEST

I'm going to scratch a particular part of my body, then sniff my fingers and describe the delightful odour. See if you can guess each of the body areas correctly. . .

B: ARMPIT

A: SOLE OF FOOT

C: UNDER SPINAL FIN

D: WEBBING BETWEEN FINGERS

E: EAR WHISKERS

Smell 1. Old mouldy blue cheese with a subtle hint of monkey sweat – truly exquisite.

Smell 2. Raw sewage with an overtone of pig manure – a top notch stench.

Smell 3. A glorious combination of old fish carcass and damp pig!

Smell 4. A pungent, fusty odour, with just a whiff of souring milk. Subtle, but potently repulsive.

Smell 5. A heavenly blend of bad egg, rotting cabbage and skunk squirt.

ANSWERS

1A 2C 3E 4D 5B

Look Fester – I've got a boil on my boil!

WOW!
A double-decker pus!

What do you call a Bogeyman in beachshorts, eating his own dandruff?

A scurf bum.

What do you call a Bogey who thinks long and hard about dirt?

A filth-osopher.

MOULD'S SUNNY DAY PAGE

'STUCK INSIDE BECAUSE THE WEATHER HAS TURNED MISERABLY HOT AND DRY? TRY SOME OF THESE FUN ACTIVITIES TO PASS THE TIME.'

BOGEY COLLAGE

Mix a pot of cold slime with some common garden muck to make a nice sticky paste. Use this paste to stick different odds and ends – old scabs, belly button fluff, dandruff, nose hairs etc – on to a piece of damp card, to make a picture. Any leftovers make a great snack.

MINIATURE MOULD GARDEN

Collect together some nice soggy leftovers from the kitchen. Add some slime, sprinkle with sewer water, then place in a nice dark, warm corner of the house. Within hours a green mould will start to form.
Leave for a few days and you will have your own little mould garden.
Lovely to look at, even nicer to eat!

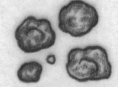

STAMP COLLECTING

See how many different slimy THINGS you can find living around your room. When you find one, stamp on it, scoop up the gloop, and save in your collecting album. If you splatter more than one of the same THINGS, see if a friend wants to do a swap.

PLAY DOUGH

Mix a cupful of filth with two cupfuls of muck, then add just enough slime to make the mixture into a sloppy, greeny-brown dough. You can use the dough to make all sorts of models, or simply tuck in.

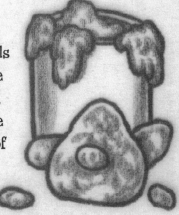

A DICTIONARY OF BOGEY

DROSSOPHILE
someone who loves decay and rot. All true Bogeys are drossophiles

FRULCH
to regurgitate partly digested food for further chewing

MUSHCACK
a paste made from mashed flatworms, usually enjoyed as a breakfast spread smeared thickly on soggy flybread

SCROFFLE
to scratch, usually in the underarm area,
so as to release body odour (hence the
phrase 'to have a good scroffle')

SWUG
to gulp slime

TRUGULOUS
slow-moving and lethargic – a complimentary
term (e.g. 'She was divine – ugly, smelly and
trugulous in all things')

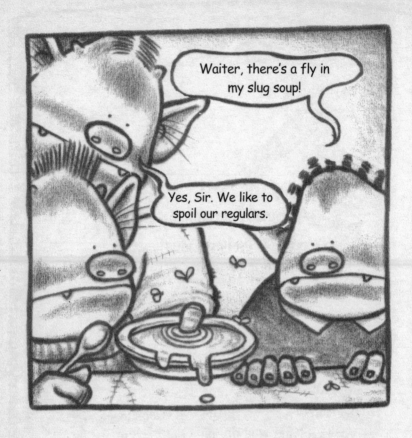

DAILY MIDDEN

PROPERTY GUIDE

GROTTLE AND BILGE ESTATE AGENTS
Dumps of Distinction, 4 Spittle Row, Slopstoc.

This delightfully damp 4-bedroomed family home,
located on the desirable Sewage Pool side of town,
boasts leaking plumbing throughout, plus well-
advanced wet rot in all ground-floor rooms.

The mature, **well-decayed** garden at the rear is dark and **damp** in all seasons, and affords an **impressive view** of the Plopland Pattyfield marshes. Many of the **dump's** original odours have been lovingly maintained.

Other attractive features include: Stinkstone mantelpiece in living room; self blocking toilets; Frigoric cooling throughout.

FOR YOUR DREAM DUMP,
LOOK FOR GROTTLE & BILGE

SOGGY PUSTATYN

Drear Fungus & family,

Having a wonderfully damp time here at the Mucklins Holiday Hulk. Wet weather every day so far, all the rancid food you can eat, and no organized outings — it's pure bliss. My room overlooks a sewage outlet — lovely. see you for a nice cold slime at the pub when we get back, Fung.

Boibye
Fester

MR. F.T. BOGEYMAN
NO. 2
THE DREGS
BOGSLOPTON
WEST TUNNELS

What do strawberries and bogies have in common?

They taste best when you pick your own.

What goes BUMP in the night?

Fungus falling out of bed.

Which country's people have, on average, the most bogies?

Boogerslavia.

FUNGUS'S FAMILY ALBUM

GRANDPA BLOAT

My father's father, a real character, famous in his time for his unrivalled ability to fart and belch simultaneously, a skill since known in the family as 'doing a Bloater'.

GRANDMA FILTHAMINA

My drear Mildew's mother, from whom she inherited her overpowering odour, deliciously damp demeanour, and flair for fetid food.

My Father

Simply the finest Bogeyman of his generation. Dad engendered over two thousand first class boils during his time, and kept a sticky upper lip, whatever the circumstances.

Cousin Crud

The black sheep of our family, who came to a non-sticky end. His failure to top up his Bogeyboots with grime led to his feet drying out, his Smell declining, and his inevitable demise. A warning to us all to avoid his deplorably dry, active, slimeless lifestyle.

The twins ~ Dank and Rank

My sister Lavatoria's two boys, slightly older than Mould, soon to sit their GCSOs (General Certificates in Sloth and Odour).

MOULD'S BOOKCASE

THE PRINCE & THE POOPER	THE THREE MUCUSTEERS	MOULDILOCKS

Pus In Boots	HARRY SNOTTER	Wind in the Pillows	Black Bogey	The Treasure Reekers

Peter Dong

Charlie and the Snot Factory

THE BURROWERS (a tale of THINGS)

Anne of Green Nostrils

The Barf is Rising

JAMES AND THE GIANT LEECH

The Adventures of Tom Sewer

What do Bogies call slimy bugs that move quickly?

Fast food.

What do you get if you cover a slug in sugar?

A Bogey sweetie.

What is Mould's favourite fizzy drink?

Slime-ade.

What should you do if a Bogeyman farts?

Run!

What happens if you play table tennis with a bad egg?

First it goes ping, then it goes pong.

How do fleas travel from Bogeyman to Bogeyman?

By itch-hiking.

FUNGUS'S FAVOURITES

'HERE ARE MY PERSONAL TOP TEN FAVOURITE THINGS. ANY OF YOURS IN THERE?'

Favourite piece of classical music –
GREENSLEEVES

Favourite type of tree –
EVERGREEN

Favourite food –
CHEESEBOOGERS

Favourite squash flavour –
LEMON AND SLIME

Favourite sweets –
CHUCKALOT ECLAIRS

Favourite love song –
ETERNAL PHLEGM

Favourite cereal –
MOULDYBIX

Favourite crisps –
*TOE CHEESE
AND BUNION*

Favourite book –
*THE SLIME MACHINE,
BY H.G. SMELLS*

Favourite cake –
MUCKAROONS

ASK FUNGUS

YOUR GREEN-FINGERED FRIEND
ANSWERS YOUR BOGEY
GARDENING QUESTIONS.

Year after year, I have problems with blooming flowers invading my manure border. Is there anything I can do?

Unfortunately, there's no quick fix for recurring flower growth – you simply have to keep pulling them up (make sure you get the roots out) or smothering them with a filth mulch.

I'd like to try growing stuff to eat in my garden. Any suggestions?

Snails or slugs are good straightforward crops for the beginner. Space them about a foot apart in a nice damp bed, and cover with a few inches of rotting rubbish. Water them regularly, and within a month you should be able to harvest enough to feed the family.

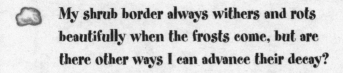 **My shrub border always withers and rots beautifully when the frosts come, but are there other ways I can advance their decay?**

Spraying with BogeyBio (concentrated night-soil) is a great way to encourage slow, foul-scented rotting of most shrubs.

I'm thinking of adding a water-feature to my small back garden. Any advice?

A cesspool not only looks good, but smells good too. If you're keen to have fish, throw in a few dead ones. Remember to add silt and filth regularly.

Brought to you by **GROLESS™**,
the Bogey Gardener's choice.

SALIVIA'S UGLY TIPS

'LOOKING THIS BAD NEEDN'T TAKE LOTS OF TIME OR EFFORT.'

NAILS
Should be short and filthy – a regular manure-icure is a must.

HAIR
Applying fish oil is a great way to keep your hair looking and smelling great.

SKIN
Aim to keep it slack, and keep it slimy – and remember, the boys like a nice boil.

YOUR SMELL
Above all, think stink. Lose your stench, and you may lose your Bogeyman.

AND THE UGLY PRODUCTS ON SALIVIA'S SHELVES...

SNAIL TRAIL HAIR GEL

SLUG SLUDGE SHAMPOO:
for greasy, lank hair – every time

LIPSLICK: mucus green

PATTY PACK:
cow dung face mask

TOOTHPUS: original
wombat's underarm flavour

DENTAL DROSS – earwaxed

ROLL-ON ODOURANT

PIGSWEAT MOUTHWASH

JUST DUST: body talc

VERRUCA CREAM: brings
them on a treat

MORE ODIOUS ODES

A BOGEY LULLABY

Hush little Bogey, don't you cry,
Daddy's gonna bake you a dead slug pie,
And if that dead slug pie's too hot
Daddy's gonna smear it with runny snot
And if that pie's not sticky enough
Daddy's gonna spray it with slimy stuff
And if that slime doesn't keep it cold
Daddy's gonna coat it in rancid mould
So hush little Bogey, don't you cry,
Daddy's gonna bake you a dead slug pie.

III

TO A FART

O what sweet stench do I detect?
  What odour so divine?
I felt a rumble down below ...
  It must be one of mine!

Such pungency, such putridness,
  It makes my spirit swell
I'm truly chuffed that when I guffed
  I brought forth such a smell.

And – joy sublime – I know for sure
  From the bubbling in my bum
    That odious fart was just the start
  I've plenty more to come!

IV

52

I've just been to buy some filth.

Expensive?

No, dirt cheap.

What does a young boil use to travel cheaply?

His pus pass.

Why do Bogies fit their graveyards with sprinklers?

To dampen their spirits.

1 SNAILEXTRIC

Race your favourite slug or snail
against your friends' on this cool
Snailextric track. Includes hi-grip
gloop-the-loop, and Eat The Winner
game rules.

cat no 277/9872

2499 BOGLES

2 BABY BARF

The only doll that cries, wets herself
and throws up. Comes with three
stained outfits.

cat no 332/4121

1499 BOGLES

3 INACTION BOGEY

Whatever the mission, Inaction
Bogey is too lazy to move.
'Inaction HQ' starter set includes
inaction figure, bed, sofa.

cat no 559/8725

1499 BOGLES

4 GIANT POOMERANG

A classic throwing toy,
made entirely of manure. Comes
back every time!
cat no 165/1662
499 BOGLES

5 LIMITED EDITION BOGEYBALL

The soggiest, stickiest ball
around, guaranteed to land
with a SPLAT every time.
cat no 347/1462
899 BOGLES

6 MUCKANNO

If you can dream it,
you can build it with Muckanno,
the only construction toy made
from 100% muck.
cat no 592/2217
1999 BOGLES

Putrid Proverbs

HOME IS WHERE THE FART IS

SLIME IS OF THE ESSENCE

THERE'S NO SLIME LIKE THE PRESENT

A STENCH IN TIME SAVES NINE

SMELLS SPEAK LOUDER THAN WORDS

ALL GOOD **THINGS** MUST COME TO AN END

THE BEST **THINGS** IN LIFE ARE GREEN

IF YOU SCRATCH MY SPINAL FIN, I'LL SCRATCH YOURS

THESE **THINGS** WERE SENT TO TRY OUT

HOME, WET HOME

What are road surfaces in Bogeydom made from?

Tarmuck.

Did you hear about that very spotty boy who didn't know what all the pus was about?

What's Fester's favourite Bogeyvision programme?

Grimewatch.

BOGEYOLOGY FOR BEGINNERS

MOULDICATING

This straightforward technique is the one most often used to introduce decay to a Drycleaner's kitchen or pantry. Simply smear foodstuffs with a thin coating of the juices that drip from within your Bogey Bag. This will bring about rapid mould growth and rot, which, strange as it may seem, will displease the Drycleaner.

MAGGOT-PLANTING

An essential technique for defiling the fruit bowl of a sleeping Drycleaner. Carried out with a custom-designed tool – a thin metal corer. Simply load with a live maggot, pierce the fruit, twist, and remove. This deposits the maggot within the fruit at precisely the correct depth to be bitten in half.

USE OF THE BOGEY STICK –
BASIC GRIPS

THE STANDARD CLASP

Used to hold the hooked end of
the **BOGEY STICK** for most
horripilation techniques –
including prodding sleeping
babies, tapping on windows,
thumping and banging etc.

THE HOOKSTICK HOLD

Used when the curved end of
the **BOGEY STICK** is required,
for such activities as filth-flicking,
lowering THINGS from above,
tripping sleepwalkers, introducing
THINGS into a toilet U-bend, etc.

THE MIDSTAFF GRIP

A light two-fingered grip for
suspending the **BOGEY STICK**
when it is being used to divine the
location of the nearest Tunnel entrance,
or Moisture Source.

62

BOGEY ETIQUETTE –

LESSON ONE: EATING OUT

TAKE YOUR BOOTS OFF ON ARRIVAL

This allows other diners to savour the putrid smell of your toe-cheese as they eat - the height of politeness. Emptying the grume and gleet from your boots on the table, for all to enjoy, also shows impeccable manners - but be sure to refill them later.

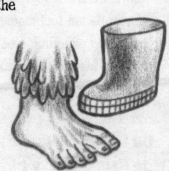

DON'T BELCH AT THE TABLE

Fart instead. Farting shows much greater appreciation for your food than belching, and helps to create a suitably rancid atmosphere for after-dinner chat. Politeness demands that you let rip after each course, at the very least.

63

DON'T WIPE YOUR NOSE ON YOUR SLEEVE

A dripping nose is very attractive. However, if the flow becomes too much, the polite things to do is wipe it on the tablecloth.

KEEP YOUR ELBOWS OFF THE TABLE

There's unlikely to be much grime or filth on your elbows, so they will add little to the tablecloth's stench. Better to show your generosity and good upbringing by wiping your underarms or feet on the tabletop, when the opportunity presents itself.

DON'T TALK WITH YOUR MOUTH FULL

If you've something to say mid-mouthful, regurgitate your food on to your plate. You can then speak clearly, and offer everyone a pleasant view of your half-chewed foodball.

What is Fungus's favourite James Bond film?

Mouldfinger.

What is the scientific name for a cluster of eight boils?

An octo-pus.

What is Mildew's favourite love song?

Slime After Slime.

FUNGUS'S PUZZLE CORNER

'A DOZEN GALLONS OF SLIME GO TO THE TOP SCORER'

 QUESTION: If it takes one Bogeyman ten minutes to clear away a heap of manure, how long would it take three Bogeymen to clear away twice as much?

 ANSWER: It depends how fast they chew it

 QUESTION: If I start out with thirty buckets of sick, then double them, what have I got?

 ANSWER: Sixty sicks

 QUESTION: What does six snails in one hand and five in the other make?

 ANSWER: Elevenses

QUESTION: I have a bag with fifteen THINGS in. I put my hand in to take four out. What am I left with?

 ANSWER: No fingers

 QUESTION: I have a bucket full of dirt, which I want to last from Monday to Friday. How much can I eat each day?

 ANSWER: A filth

 QUESTION: I have sixteen slugs, and I want to give half to my friend. What should I do?

 ANSWER: Spit eight of them back out

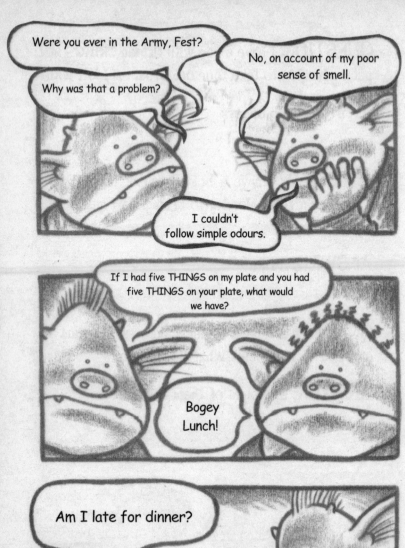

Boogerbooks.co.tun

If you enjoyed this book, why not try one of our other top titles:

101 THINGS TO DO WITH THINGS
Advanced Bogeyology for those who want to be a bit more inventive with the contents of their Bogey Bag.

TIPS FOR UP TOP – A SURVIVOR'S GUIDE
Author Scab Sourcrud was once trapped Up Top for five gruelling days. Here he draws on his own terrifying experience to offer advice on evading sunlight, emergency dungaree repairs, ways to keep wet, how to erect a Stench Tent and much much more.

THE SLIME OUT GUIDE TO FOOD AND DRINK
If you're looking for a repulsively filthy place to eat, where the food is truly foul and the atmosphere is rank, this book offers the ultimate guide to where's grot, and where's not.

MANURE AND MORE: A CONCISE HISTORY OF MUCK
Over ten years of painstaking, muckraking research went into producing this essential text for all budding filth historians. Illustrated throughout with lavish Bogachrome photography.

For a complete list of available titles, visit us at Boogerbooks.co.tun

That's all for now.
Bye, bye my smelly little Bogey chums.

Books by Raymond Briggs

FUNGUS THE BOGEYMAN
FATHER CHRISTMAS
THE SNOWMAN

THE FATHER CHRISTMAS
IT'S A BLOOMING TERRIBLE JOKE BOOK